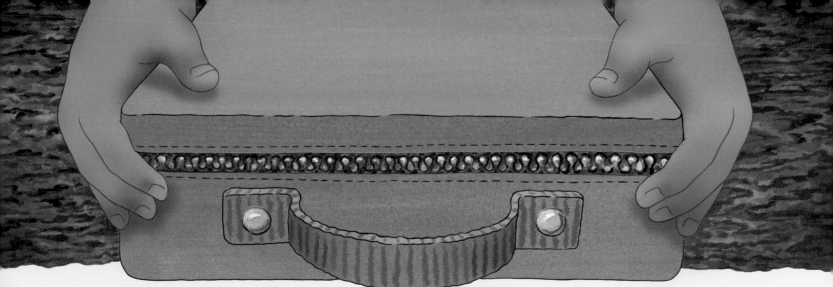

This Is NOT My Lunch Box!

In memory of my mother who brought to life the beauty found in nature and my husband who believed in me from the beginning.
—Jennifer Dupuis

To Silas, Amy, and Brixton—
I hope you find just what you want in your lunch box!
Thanks,
Carol

Library of Congress Cataloging-in-Publication Data

Names: Dupuis, Jennifer, author. | Schwartz, Carol, 1954- illustrator.
Title: This is not my lunch box! / written by Jennifer Dupuis ; illustrated by Carol Schwartz.
Description: [Ann Arbor, Michigan] : [Tilbury House Publishers], [2024] | Audience: Ages 4-10 | Summary: "Join in on a surprising camping trip and discover the favorite meals of your favorite forest creatures-from the wood frog to the moose. Rich art illustrates the beautiful biodiversity found in our forests and expressive, repetitive text helps even the youngest naturalists learn all about herbivores, omnivores, and carnivores"-- Provided by publisher.
Identifiers: LCCN 2023045404 | ISBN 9781668936856 (hardcover)
Subjects: LCSH: Forest animals--Juvenile literature. | Forest animals--Food--Juvenile literature. | Food chains (Ecology)--Juvenile literature. | Biodiversity--Juvenile literature. | Color--Juvenile literature.
Classification: LCC QL112 .D87 2024 | DDC 591.73--dc23/eng/20231204
LC record available at https://lccn.loc.gov/2023045404

TILBURY HOUSE
PUBLISHERS

an imprint of
Cherry Lake Publishing Group
2395 South Huron Parkway, Suite 200
Ann Arbor, MI 48104
www.tilburyhouse.com

Printed and bound in South Korea

10 9 8 7 6 5 4 3 2 1

This Is NOT My Lunch Box!

Written By Jennifer Dupuis

Illustrated By Carol Schwartz

Aaah . . .
camping in the forest.
My tent is up.
My sleeping bag is open.
My campfire is lit.

Time to eat. Here is my red lunch box. What have you packed for me today?

Crawling carpenter ants,

busy beetles,

spongy spiders.

No, thank you! I will **NOT** eat that! This is not my lunch box. This lunch box belongs to the . . .

DOWNY
WOODPECKER

Time to eat. Here is my green lunch box. What have you packed for me today?

Gnarly nuts, wiggling worms, tangy truffles.

No, thank you! I will **NOT** eat that! This is not my lunch box. This lunch box belongs to the . . .

JUMPING
MOUSE

Time to eat. Here is my white lunch box. What have you packed for me today?

Clean clover,

assorted acorns,

sweet strawberries.

No, thank you! I will **NOT** eat that! This is not my lunch box. This lunch box belongs to the . . .

BLACK BEAR

Time to eat. Here is my purple lunch box. What have you packed for me today?

Fuzzy flies,

angry aphids,

meaty moths.

No, thank you! I will **NOT** eat that! This is not my lunch box. This lunch box belongs to the . . .

PRAYING MANTIS

Time to eat. Here is my brown lunch box. What have you packed for me today?

Pungent pondweed,

bitter bark,

shrouded shrubs.

No, thank you! I will **NOT** eat that! This is not my lunch box. This lunch box belongs to the . . .

MOOSE

Time to eat. Here is my yellow lunch box. What have you packed for me today?

Slimy snails,

scurrying spiders,

every kind of egg.

No, thank you! I will **NOT** eat that! This is not my lunch box. This lunch box belongs to the . . .

WOOD
FROG

Time to eat. Here is my pink lunch box. What have you packed for me today?

frosty fruit,

Racing rodents,

flopping fish.

No, thank you! I will **NOT** eat that!

This is not my lunch box. This lunch box belongs to the . . .

RED FOX

Time to eat. Here is my gray lunch box. What have you packed for me today?

Mushy mealworms,

gritty grains,

colorful crab apples.

No, thank you! I will **NOT** eat that!
This is not my lunch box.
This lunch box belongs to the . . .

AMERICAN
ROBIN

Time to eat. Here is my orange lunch box. What have you packed for me today?

Busy bees,

mischievous moles,

whizzing wasps.

No, thank you! I will **NOT** eat that!
This is not my lunch box.
This lunch box belongs to the . . .

SKUNK

Time to eat. Here is my blue lunch box. What have you packed for me today?

Lurking larvae,

prancing pollen,

nourishing nectar.

No, thank you! I will **NOT** eat that! This is not my lunch box. This lunch box belongs to the . . .

LIGHTNING BUG

Time to eat. Here is my black lunch box. What have you packed for me today?

Festive fungi,

crackling corn,

luscious lichens.

No, thank you!
I will **NOT** eat that!
This is not my lunch box.
This lunch box belongs to the . . .

WHITE-TAILED
DEER

Time to eat. Here is my rainbow lunch box. What have you packed for me today?

Welcome water,

a purple plum,

yummy yogurt,

a crisp cucumber,

crunchy crackers.

Yes, please!
Yes, please!
I **WILL** eat this!
This lunch box belongs to . . .

ME!

What is in *your* lunch box?

WHAT AM I?

Match each animal on the next page with its eating habits!

I am an *herbivore*, an animal that eats fruits and
vegetables, leaves, seeds, and grasses to live.

I am a *carnivore*, an animal that eats other animals to live.

I am an *omnivore*, an animal that eats both plants and animals to live.

Jennifer Dupuis is a blind children's book author who enjoys beekeeping, ballroom dancing, and playing her guitar for anyone who will listen. You can find her YouTube channel at "Living with Blindness and Balance." Having worked with children for thirty-five years, she recognizes the power of laughter in learning and thus weaves wonderful humor into all that she writes. Jennifer lives in southern Maine with her husband and two sons and is proud to have received the 2020 Evelyn Morrill Durgin Award for her years of work as a volunteer within her community.

Carol Schwartz has illustrated more than fifty picture books, including *My Busy Green Garden*, which *Kirkus* called "a lovely literary and artistic rendering." Her other books include *Sea Squares*, an Outstanding Science Trade Book and Children's Choice Award winner; *The Maiden of Northland*, an Aesop Accolade winner; and *Thinking about Ants*, an Outstanding Science Trade Book. Carol taught illustration at Milwaukee Institute of Art & Design and has shared her passion for illustrating at the hundreds of elementary schools, libraries, conferences, and colleges she has visited. She lives in Connecticut.